Office Poems

Nathan Nicolau

Table of Contents

I. Ars Politico

2014 to 2019 Poetic Sketch 4
Needle in ¾ Time 5
To a Crisis in the Film Industry 6
If E.E. Cummings Was a Cowboy... 7
Starring Scarlett Johansson as The Major... 8
Max Sang the Blues 12
Putting the Cat Down Blues 13
Transgender Lunch 14
Ben Shapiro and Alexandria Ocasio-Cortez... 15
Speeding Up the World 17

II. Harmonious Love, Chaotic Death

Love is Sharing a Bathroom 19
And This Is Another Lie 20
Love in a South Carolina Gas Station Bathroom 21
You Hide It So Well 22
They Play The Eagles in Heaven 23
Agape Found 24

III. People I Know (or Haven't Met)

Here's to Many More, Mrs. Cottrell 26
Speaking of Her Majesty Charlotte 28
Cross-Pollination 30
Touching Coltrane's Tenor Sax 31
A Saga of Wood 32
Ferlinghetti and I Share a Birthday 33
The Possibility of Multiverses 34
Looking at Gabriel 35
Lunch with Frank O'Hara at the Mexican Cantina... 38

IV. Nature's Dharma

Mindfulness 42
The Patio Outside My World 44
Hamburger Petrichor 45
Buddha Speaks Through the Water 47
Free 48
Our Beholders 49

I.

Ars Politico

2014 to 2019 Poetic Sketch

(In Spirit of Frank O'Hara's "Poem")

There's a water park in Flint!
I was driving down the highway
with the kids in the back trying to find
lunch, but all the restaurants were closed,
and here comes the tall plastic slides looking
so dry, and that's when I shouted
There's a water park in Flint!
And then the kids asked why
wouldn't there be a water park in Flint,
and I asked if they wanted a water bottle,
and they said no, but it wasn't for drinking,
it was for swimming because
<u>There's a water park in Flint</u>
and we're going to play there.
Splash splish sploosh glug glug.
Want this empty bottle?

Needle in ¾ Time

Sewing is one of those things I can't do
          (In-out-in-out-in-out-in-out-in)
because putting the needle in my hand would make
me question.   (out-in-out-in-out-in-out-in-out)
I jab the needle into my palm
and wiggle it around to make sure it's still there.
I would ask myself   (in-in-out)   why I would do
                    (out-in-in) that,
and for what effect than to ask
why   (out-out) God didn't stop me.

Better my hand
          (out-in-in)   than another's,
transferring my blood to someone   (out-in-in)   who
won't need it.
I love my brothers too much;
I used a Butterfly needle so it wouldn't hurt.
                    (in-
                              out-
                              out-
                    in-
                              out-
                              out)
He's smiling (in) on me. He sure is (out).

To a Crisis in the Film Industry

Cinema provocateur Jean-Luc Godard was found dead this morning at the (bloody) hands of Chantel Ackerman. Police discovered the knife from between Godard's legs (and took great precaution in reinserting it) to prevent further bleeding. Local film students will hold the funeral in Paris under the same stars (and police sirens) Godard slept under. There will be a screening of *Jeanne Dielman, 23 quai du Commerce, 1080 Bruxelles* (the Criterion Blu-Ray, as always) in honor of Ackerman (with a live performance of the final scene), but attendance is mandatory. When asked to comment, Scorsese put on a (spandex) mask and laughed (while shooting the scene up).

If E.E. Cummings Was a Cowboy, There Would Be a Whole Lot of Dead Horses

Actually,
Buffalo Bill
        never came riding—
        he took a breather at the local bp station to douse
$5 gasoline on the kids.
Stopping him would be like explaining
                                                                        Dali
to someone with synesthesia.
        But even then, all you would have to say is

                                                                    no

Starring Scarlett Johansson as The Major in 2017's *Ghost in the Shell*

What dreams can I talk about today, Scarlett? You and the other angels live out yours: to play as any person that does their taxes. How I envy! A supposedly Japanese cyborg doesn't have to use its walkie-talkie telepathic gizmo to call the IRS. You think the screenwriter who came up with that plot point had a scene where the protagonist filled out a 1040? The phone rings:

> "My wife's leaving. We need something to actually happen in this here *pick-tchah*. Move the setting to D.C. on January 6th. Have her screw a blonde and put a hole thru a terrorist's head. No guns in D.C.? The hell ya talking about? I believe that more than the blonde."

(Sir, your 2 p.m. is ready.)

> "What happened to the footage I was supposed to get yesterday? I need fresh, I need hot, I need to go back to the time where my job was fun. The skirts are getting longer. The men are getting skinnier. I

didn't suffer through a Capra movie for this. Book that room."

(EXT. THE HOLY LAND - NIGHT)

Our hero, a dog on the streets, thirstier for success than Horatio Alger. His foil, "the woman," rips off the heels of her shoes to run faster. **By the way, for those of you jotting down notes in your Moleskin notebooks: you can't suddenly turn high-heels into flats. For the amount of time you all look at women's legs, you'd think you'd realize how strong they are to run 0-60mph** The sheep flying over remind them how children's skin makes for good furniture.

"Where's the slaves? Where's the slaves, man? I can't sell this in China. Don't you want the gold? You people lack ambition. How can you come into this country, get thousands of dollars in debt at UCLA, then send something like this to me? I said no camera in the rooms, dear."

<u>Cut!</u>

check the gate we broke the line but we'll fix it in post hey you—

(My name only has 6 letters.)

whatever grab that mighty mole off the beefy baby triple riser and hold up the buttplug with C-47's the HMC needs fluid the bag of T-stops is next to it triple time 2 creams 2 sugars a shot of Grey Goose and an American Spirit Abbey Singer then send the dailies over

(Please speak English for once.)

are you an American you're not an American I can smell you from the crafty table good luck cleaning toilets while I actually do something with my life my orange juice was warm by the way there's some rope on the prop table see if it fits you

NOTES FOR THE EDITOR:

Cut the opening crawl. They're getting too smart.
Raise the mix or I will end you.
Stay in your lane.
Lighten the skin tones.
Change your name to something Spanish.

It's 11 p.m. now. I got a plane to catch at dawn, and I'm still sitting at a bar in Hollywood that serves omelets for 20 bucks with people I'll never see again—including that security guard waiting outside the bathrooms for some no-name to come out. Who's going to hurt you when no one cares? In that case, let's give every bum in Santa Monica a guy with a gun that isn't a cop. I was waiting for my Lyft outside (anyone here can tell you Uber is for fascists) when that security guard stepped out, complimented my sneakers, and asked if he could clean them. He kept his eyes off Scarlett when that Uber came barreling by (see?) and then she stepped inside and

> oh my god Scarlett this can't be
> we loved you so
> you were great with bill murray
> say hello to Mrs. Wood
> catch
> kill
> next

Max Sang the Blues

max sang the blues while moose the mooche got off easy speeding through every red light in LA to the convenience store for Slurpees taquitos and redemption max and moose go way back 15 minutes ago at one of those classic California shindigs where you had to know someone who knew someone who knew someone who knew you even though they still get your name wrong and it's only 3 letters pick your favorite bebop tune nothing under 250 bpm moose rattled like a Keuro-*back* character jump jivin' about cat's swingin' turkey talk about wickywickywhackywoo women over a slow risin' mornin' and don't forget the cigarette lucky strikes as always max didn't want the blues but who does moose is on the hov lane scatting away a bird line backwards talking about drugs he's never taken and fights he wish he had max just wished he'd shut up but moose was the guy who knew someone who knew someone who knew max so it's too late now they're on the hov lane *you ain't never had to cry baby don't start cryin' now*

Putting the Cat Down Blues

Could you imagine
if everyone that complained about free things
in life had to hand over the keys to their
golf carts?
Then we wouldn't have any more shattered windows,
stray golf balls in my living room,
and no more
"Would you like to be in the room when it
happens?"

Transgender Lunch

What's new at the tattoo parlors?
How many flags that we pray to
can fit on human skin?
Suppose we write yesterday's manifesto
on our backs so that when we pretend
to strut away from the world,
people can read it in full for once
instead of being on their phones thinking
we want transgender lunches—
pineappleroastbeefhotdogs!

Ben Shapiro and Alexandria Ocasio-Cortez on the South Border of Texas

Here's a headline for you:
I'm young! I'm hip! I'm easy! What do I know?
Tell me!
I know how to say "no" in 20 different languages and only nine
(German)
of them can I use.
Did you know there's no way to say "no" in Texas?
Coat sales are up because of it, and it's not even winter.
Just buy the ugliest Grandma coat you can and throw it to the orphans.
The hanger is a hot commodity. Why do they make them so cheap now?
Plastic doesn't feel good on skin, and metal tastes better.
Anyway, if I say "no," not only will people hear me,
but I'll get a couple of Facebook posts,
a truck to take me home,
and a free appearance on Fox News as a consolation prize.
Make sure my hair's dyed. People have to know who I voted for.
They need a good target from 6 feet away.
I prefer red. It'll match my FTM packer.
What's an FTM packer?
The Arctic Monkey's fourth album.

Did you hear AOC OD'd FDA's PCP GOP?
        Rant about it in the car.
                I'll get the camera; you get the guns.
I'll put the ring light above you so people can see the spit flying.
        Turn up the heat in here.
                You love the winter—the snowflakes fall.
                I hate the winter—the bodies freeze over.

Speeding Up the World

Drink your coffee at 2 a.m.
and read the news before anyone else.
That way, you'd be the first to comment
before they put another stopper on you.
Never look at clocks—they haven't changed much.
If you're like me who was never good at math,
you would think clocks would go by events,
not intervals. Instead, sit out at the park with a loved one,
and assess all your hopes.
"Assess" might be too clinical, so try prayer instead.
"Prayer" might be too uncertain,
so maybe fall asleep after that 2 a.m. coffee
and wake up a day faster with
no more worries for tomorrow.
The truth is that we're all bullets for someone's gun.
So, send those postcards before the first one grazes us.

II.

Harmonious Love, Chaotic Death

Love is Sharing a Bathroom

and I also think it's about the eyes
on you behind the shower curtains, doing
a cute little hug to distract them from the toilet—
which people never saw outside their homes and bars
and offices until the release of the movie *Psycho* in 1960.
Perhaps it's strange to mention love, toilets,
and *Psycho* in the same verse, and there's
a joke in there somewhere about love being crazy,
but a joke can't sum up anything—much like how
people grumble, "you can't joke about anything nowadays,"
but there's plenty we can joke about with someone
we share a bathroom with:
    The waitress's thick accent at dinner.
    The spotless houses the characters in rom-coms have.
    The reason why women's pants don't have pockets.
But until 1960, people didn't want to talk about a toilet.
I'm glad times have changed because I hope
people know that heart-swelling feeling
when you're on the toilet while your partner is brushing
their teeth and you tell a joke so dumb their toothpaste
splatters on the mirror,
and then when you go up to clean it, they flush for you.

And This Is Another Lie

If I tell you I hate you, hold it against me
as the others did with their venomous tongues.
If I tell you I can survive, starve me from the sun
and feed me to the heartbroken artists
making their elephant's graveyards around
yet another stranded dead romantic before their time.

If I tell you that my poems aren't for you,
tell everyone that when someone enters a poem
they can't be there to cry, bleed, reflect, pray, or apologize.
If I tell you that when someone enters a poem
there can't be fanfare or a twist—
that they simply cannot be there
because people simply don't exist for others—
at that point, pull the plug
and put a toaster in the socket instead.

Someone—a God, a government, or a concerned parent—
put you and me in this house together as punishment.
And wouldn't it be awful if I went to an eternal hell
where I all did was listen to your heartbeat
and take pictures
and eat all your chow mein I want.

Love in a South Carolina Gas Station Bathroom

Written in dark black graffiti
next to the once
stainless porcelain seats
now turned a pale shade of yellow
in between the maroon and brown
covered walls thick with grease
and below the dusty sinks
sprinkled with gray ashes
were the words
Love is a consequence

You Hide it So Well

But what does that mean? That I'm an excellent illusion or the perfect alibi? Never forget that the soul's void still has a vibrant color—the same as my nails after a biting session. Fingernails have such a distinct flavor. I prefer dipping them in hand sanitizer so that when it hits my tongue, it jolts me out of the cerebral dungeon. Every writer talks about depression and anxiety (they're both as natural as drinking), but they're such boring things to write about because most of the time, I'm just taking breaths like anyone else. But I have to count mine just how my therapist, the internet, and all my angry bosses told me. I saw a movie where a character said, "I had depression," and even though I hate to laugh at a person's misfortune, I don't think the person who wrote that line ever had to take citalopram (and I doubt he knows how to say it). Here's where I'm getting at: I walked through a bookstore recently and found one book that called depression a magic trick, and even though I wanted to curse out that sales lady at the mall for that sneering look and use that book as my alibi, wouldn't it be too inhuman of me to stop my breathing? No one would have ever guessed.

They Play The Eagles in Heaven

(for Alfred "Skip" Ehrenstein)

I used to drive him home late at night
after poker games and a few beers
and he would sing "The Best Of My Love"
silently, as if he didn't want me to listen
even though I liked that song too.
Typically he would spin into his
usual banter about the Air Force,
old buds, Redskin games, and life lessons,
but as the streetlamps guided us home,
he sang the whole song with his eyes closed,
not another word to me except
"Good night," after an "I love you."
Months later, when he landed in the hospital
for what was going to be the last time
he said the first thing he wanted when he leaves
was a good cheeseburger and a beer.
I said, "I love you."
He said, "Don't do anything I wouldn't do."
I didn't want to leave it like that, but that's how he was.
A text message greeted me when I went home:
A YouTube link. "The Best Of My Love." The Eagles.
released in 1974 from their album On the Border.
From then on, I stopped saying "I love you"
because he wouldn't do that.
I started showing love instead.

Agape Found

(for Elizabeth Nicolau)

No one is perfect, but I wanted to be.
Obtaining the unobtainable is a faithful leap,

and faith is what holds me to you.
Memories are only dreams we believe in.

And what a beautiful dream this is to blink every day
and see you for the first time just like our daughter.

III.

People I Know (or Haven't Met)

Here's to Many More, Mrs. Cottrell

I owe my
life to my
mother, but I
owe my career
to Mrs. Cottrell,
the self-proclaimed
wicked witch of
fourth-grade teachers.
I just learned
how to spell
my last name
and here she
comes staring me
down with her
wide red eyes
asking me why
my poem about
the Titanic sinking
didn't rhyme and
I said I
couldn't find anything
that rhymed with
"sunked" (and no
one corrected me
until high school)

and her chameleon
eyes whizzed around,
her tongue swishing
that I'll never
see next year.
Well, it's a
another night in
my apartment with
my wife and
our baby and
my two cats,
and I need
to wake up
early to go
teach college freshmen,
who wince at
the name "literature,"
the why of
poetry instead of
the how. See
you next year.

Speaking of Her Majesty Charlotte

Next to you and all the other worlds you contain
(like Uptown and Noda and University City),
I find solace in looking at the rush hour traffic as much as
you do. I can't name another city where even the homeless
smile, wave, and open doors for you. And it seems harder
than ever to find a place to get decent BBQ,
but the homely people over at Tent City will give you some
of theirs.

I look up at the Bank of America tower
(the place where my mother spent countless nights keeping
you and me alive),
and I wonder if this will be the same view that will keep me
writing in my empty notebook.
I'd rather look around the Uptown Mint Museum
than all the castles in the world, mainly because the Mint
has Romare Bearden, but also because those castles lack
street art.

And speaking of street art,
the ones in Noda could wake anybody up with their colors.
That and the mix of incense trailing down the street
leading you to the oddity shops could make even a
non-believer walk away with Buddha or Vishnu or God or
whoever you want to cry to.

And I'm not sure what the other queen Ella Fitzgerald
was talking about with Mott Street in July,
but what street could ever compare to South Tryon during
lunchtime? I've had too many lunches shoving down
hotdogs and sushi with Bearden, and I'd probably do the
same in New York anyway, so there's that.

What I'm getting at is that by morning
I'll be farther from your royal touch,
and I'd love to spend another wonderful night with you.
I'll accompany you to see the court jesters at Blumenthal
with you, and have a street-lit dinner at the halal food truck
next door—just name a date and time; the Lynx Blue Line
awaits.

Cross-Pollination

Debussy's piano sounds like a painting,
possibly a Monet, definitely not a Dali,
but ever-so-slightly a Van Gogh.

This is the only music where the office turns into watercolors. The overhead lights are too bright, the white concrete walls are musty, the brown-stained microwave is possessed with rage. Debussy's harp plasters over it all with pastels. I wait for it every day after lunch, but now it's 1:04 p.m., and the lights are buzzing loud, and the poets are going quiet. I have a few emails to read, but none of them is a libretto worthy of Schiele, so why bother?

I called Brenden to see what the New Jersey rappers are into now. They're the new composers—the new paint to fill my office days.

The backbeat starts another feeling I can't shake—to live in a painted world while the wistful glitch synths champion my successes and cry for my misfortunes. Other's souls lifted by noise fill my heart as I walk, fly, and sail through my room—a blank canvas in a museum of hope.

1:25 p.m. Five minutes left until I leave.
One last color:
the silence.

Touching Coltrane's Tenor Sax

(an apology to the NC Music Hall of Fame)

I had to feel his brass body while no one was looking.
The electric shock I felt from my fingers to my heart
matched the passions I heard from this sax so many times.

> Across from him was Monk, but they sold his piano
> for one of his records—so I couldn't bounce on his
> keys, sadly. But the way Nina Simone swaddled the
> pearls around her neck so soft, so cool, reminded
> me how I should feel (*birds flying high, you know*).

I'd like to add all this to that list next to those raindrops,
whiskers,

brown pa *per* *pack* *aaaage*
eee *ss*
tied up
with *strii* *ii* *iings.*

When I drove home, I put on that album.
Oh, wait. He played the soprano. Where is that?

A Saga of Wood

(A Confession to Walt Whitman)

And then the big American with the white beard said,

"I am not a force of nature,
I am the nature of force.
For I am like God; I destroy this Earth I create.
I speak in enigmas; none can discern me.
You who speak delusions!
Why must you use my creation beyond its purpose?
My heavenly touch forged this wood for man;
not for man to forge with wood.
Your houses, your tools, your fires, your frames,
your chairs, your limbs; from wood they arise.
Your manuals, your treatises, your rants, your letters of love
and gratitude and hurt, your lies, your confirmations
From wood they arise!
Make no mistake:
Nothing must be wasted!
Nothing shall be lost!
Come to me, you poets, you liars, your dogs,
your cheats, you scoundrels, you killers of time.
Take your hands and place them upon
my touch to burn the forests of your mind!"

And then some poet probably woke up and yawned.

Ferlinghetti and I Share a Birthday

I'm not going to wax poetically about it
because what kind of a hack would I be?
The only poetic line I'll crack is this:

You and I never met, and by the time
I was told to pray to you,
you were a 100-year-old sage

speaking our common language,
sharing our friends,
and hustling this untapped market called poetic verse.

But anyway, what I'll also say is
next time some "dame"
(we call them "ladies" now, Lawrence)

Comes in hating poetry,
let's play the jazz louder
or the theatrics softer.

Or even better, let's talk about how
you share a birthday with Houdini,
who I now call the second greatest illusionist.

The Possibility of Multiverses

Seeing other worlds in my

cat leads to a dogmatic

future of ransacked dreams.

I never saw her as a kitten.

Looking at Gabriel

(for Gabby Johnson)

Light and fog swirling into an everlasting night.
The swishing of brushes, an open sea.
The color of their wings, pure as choirs.

Spirits are not absolute.
They are not a guardian.
They are not refugees.

They are a listener—
a comforter—
an amplifier of expression.

Jazz is the closest thing we have
to speaking in tongues.
Only those gifted can talk.

But their words come out too shallow,
too spiteful for our fathers to listen.
That's why we are damned in light.

Jazz is played in groups but felt alone.
The tears inside.
Their smiles shadow someone else.

There's a genealogy of soul
stretching back to the time when
people cried for their mothers.

Back when people died for this music,
they wander now, looking for each other.
Lost in their own prejudices.

Are we slaves to our past?
Is predetermination a curse?
What does it matter?

The moon is too high
to answer questions like that.
Let that night close us out.

Our moments cannot be wasted
on old thoughts, old friends, old traditions—
but if only it was that easy.

We empty our minds until it all ends.
That's why we're all here listening
to the winged man on stage crying.

He can't speak our native language.
That's why his sobs come out

from a mouthful of brass.

His glassy eyes pierce us.
He would renounce it all like his brethren
just to hold us in his arms once more, to shield us.

Only he sees the cages locked by our pasts.
It angers him, but it has to be so.
This is what makes us different from our creator.

But every so often, just as predicted,
a shepherdless lamb comes to rest
in this crowd beyond the stage.

He listens to Gabriel's song
and dreams of a new future,
one not soiled by a path determined.

Gabriel plays softer
and softer
and softer for them.

Lunch with Frank O'Hara at the Mexican Cantina: Selected and Abridged

A quick poem while he's eating—
I passed Frank the napkin and
he only wrote a few words:

Man

what a

life

Whitman wrote the same thing last week—
Frank didn't laugh.
We shared the chips and salsa.
It wasn't hot enough.
We'd drink it like our 3rd cup of coffee this morning.
The senorita in the white blouse gave
him the eye. Frank laughed. I turned
his pages.
Lana Turner?

He's about to speak to me again.
I grabbed the napkin.
Kerouac? Don't bother.
You need a beat for jazz but not a Beat for poetry.

I see you,

Frank

I hear your

laugh

I think about

you
whenever I take a dump at church as you told me.
I'd take you with, but they told me you're no good.
What do they know? Those old ladies are gonna pass on a Sunday anyway.
(This burrito is gonna go right through me.)

Lana brought the check.
She eyes my Frank again.
They share a smile after a glance,
talking about which place in New York City is
the best to catch a concert and a smoke.
I've been under the city lights with Frank
and I can't come close to the way his
flamenco-tinged language gave the night
to a lady named Day.

I'd love to just grab a cigarette,
light it, and burn it off on a white
page as he does. But I need my lungs
to vent, to love, to dance to bebop.
If I read the O'Hara Monogatari,

would I even recognize it? Would
others recognize me?

I looked at the napkin. You're right, Frank.
See you at 12 p.m. You forgot your leftovers.

IV.

Nature's Dharma

Mindfulness

Twilight outside my window,
and here I am sitting while writing about
Zen monks who always took a walk
around a time like this.

I, like any other poet,
write about rivers with flowers
and animals that have rivers
with flowers in their eyes.
But I don't feel the coolness
of those waters. I don't smell
the nectar of God's creation.
Truth, as I knew that word,
comes from a past life with
an absolute future.
If the present moment wanted
to be known why hasn't it jumped
out of its axel like the wheels on a cart?
Outside always was and will be.
I do not need to go out
and confirm the truth.

But then I look at the cart's
wheels in my mind.

In each wheel, spokes extend from the center, reaching out
to its circular path.
The middle: solid matter,
stuck in a void to only give balance.
Yet between every spoke, nothingness takes the form of negative space,
connecting both the circle and the center.
This is it.
This is natural.
This is purpose.

And it was now that I realized
while taking up my brush
that the wiseness of those Zen monks,
their words and minds flowing
from one nature to the next,
did not come from education.
It came from the outside in.
Outside, I breathe,
turning the doorknob.

The Patio Outside My World

The hummingbird came as I read Buddha's words about awareness, how awareness leads us to an island so proud that no flood could reach. The hummingbird hungers, but I had no food to give. All I had were the violets on my island, which she was more than welcome to. But now, the worker bee floats across, seeking rest for all his hard work. The hummingbird stops, sees the bee meditate on my violets, and leaves. A verse comes to me:

The wind, its chime
        as soft as jazz—
                the birds responding,
                        allowing silence.

If only Earth was paradise now.

Hamburger Petrichor

(for Nina Tungjairob)

I'm sorry for writing so late.

I was at the beach and Posiden's horses took my glasses back to their kingdom and I was so mad, but I figured I didn't have to see anyway because CNN showed something so disgusting this morning.

Could you believe that there are people who breathe the same air as us that can't pronounce our ancestor's home correctly? It's not "thigh-land" but "tie," like the only thing that pulls us together through all this yelling and food poisoning and passive-aggressive phone calls around our family.

I'm telling you, cousin, I'm losing it.

I wish people understood things the same way I understood how you wanted me to write about the smell of rain and hamburgers outside my home, something so coincidental, so minute, that I had to laugh.

I thought it wouldn't make sense, that it couldn't be done, that I was wasting my time and you were just teasing me.

Then I got that Buddha necklace from you that I still had on me even while in the ocean (the horses steered away from it), and that's when I had my epiphany, my Buddha-lying-sideways-dying moment, that our world is full of conflicting things that I can't see but others can smell, and even nature was begging me to see that.

I'm practically blind without my glasses, but Buddha's eyes are always closed, smelling the Earth, connecting nature to you and to me through rain and hamburgers.

Buddha Speaks Through The Water

I offered him water at his alter this morning.
“The fountain needs only four coins—
    for today’s sun,
    for those who clean our fountains,
    for the ones not here,
    for the fortune of the swimming ducks.”
I left home with five.

Free

The
tide
pulls
forward
as
a
stampede
of
horses.

They charge ahead,
disperse all around,
and then retreat.

Come
back.

Our Beholders

I.

The people who remember to take pictures
are the ones I envy the most.
Remembering to remember remembering,
a dream's sonata cycling through nature.
I stare at this flower to judge if it's worth looking at.
The colors duller than I see in pictures,
the stem leaning down in sobbing prayer,
its petals dry from a relentless summer.
Our vision cannot be an absolute truth,
I ponder as I pick this flower from its stem.
But as I look up and see the colorful sea
only to look down at this drifted island I've created,
I had to raise my lens.

II.

With how many songs about love there are,
you'd think we'd care more about the mushrooms
that come up from the ground to kiss us.
Love songs are about stealing kisses away from the world,
yet there are no lyrics about kissing a mushroom.
How unfair is it that a mushroom comes up for us to love
and we respond by grabbing her stocky body,

driving her out of her home, resting her in a freezing box,
and putting her lips on a hot pan.
Yet notice, still, as the mushroom sizzles in its oil pool,
it's not a cry, but a song. Is it a love song?
Bring your lips closer and she'll tell you.

III.

The crowd stares into the eyes of the pregnant seahorse as he dips and heaves and flies through his birthing ground. And when he pops litters of offsprings to people's cheers, a lady walks away and scoffs, "No one clapped when I did that."

ACKNOWLEDGEMENTS

This book would not be possible without the love and support of the following people. Special thanks to Mom, Dad, Isaac, and Nana, for being the most supportive family I know. And thank you, Nina Tunjairob, for being more than a cousin to me. I need to immensely thank the English faculty at UNCC for their guidance. Finally, I need to thank the two most important women in my life: Elizabeth and Avery.

I need to thank the following journals and websites for housing my work. "Needle in ¾ Time" and "Here's to Many More, Mrs. Cottrell" first appeared in NiftyLit. "Starring Scarlett Johansson as The Major in 2017's *Ghost in the Shell*" first appeared in Red Ogre Review. "Speeding up the World" first appeared in *Meniscus*. "Love is Sharing a Bathroom" first appeared in Chariot Press. "Looking at Gabriel" first appeared in Noctua Review. "Mindfulness" first appeared in Local Gem Press' *North Carolina Bards 2021 Poetry Anthology*. "A Saga of Wood" first appeared in Local Gem Press' *North Carolina Bards 2022 Poetry Anthology*. "The Patio Outside My World" first appeared in Blumenthal Art's *Of Earth and Sky* poetry anthology and art installation by Luke Jerram. "Our Beholders" first appeared in Beyond Words Literary Magazine.

ABOUT THE AUTHOR

While most kids wanted to be astronauts or firefighters when they grew up, Nathan Nicolau wanted to be a writer. Since his published debut in 2019, his fiction, poetry, and essays have been featured on numerous websites and magazines. Nathan is also the founder/editor of New Note Poetry, an online poetry magazine. He currently lives in Charlotte, NC, with his wife and daughter.

ALSO BY NATHAN NICOLAU

Goodnight Youth: Poems

Written shortly after being released from a mental hospital, this short yet eclectic collection of poems muses on two central themes that plagued Nicolau's mind: regret and love. The poems in this collection explore, deconstruct, and reaffirm these universal themes. Honest, raw, and emotionally charged, *Goodnight Yout*h marks the beginning of a promising young writer.

Nights at the Turntable: Jazz Poetry

A collection of jazz-inspired poetry by avid jazz lover and poet Nathan Nicolau. Across twenty poems, this collection pays homage to the people, places, and voices that made jazz what it is. Brimming with poetic language and heart, *Nights at the Turntable* will delight both the casual listener and the most serious jazz fans.

So Quiet this Wind: Haiku

So Quiet This Wind adds a refreshing spin on the classic haiku form while also embracing traditionalist conventions. This collection will delight all haiku lovers young and old.

Vantage Points: Flash Fictions

From acclaimed writer Nathan Nicolau comes *Vantage Points*, a flash-fiction collection about perception. Each story focuses on how a character sees the world, sees others, or how they see themselves. The stories in this collection explore different aspects of the human condition—the positives, the negatives, and even the ugly—but reframes them through the eyes of unique characters, all in 1,000 words or less.

ISBN: 978-93-95224-71-0

First Edition: 2023
Rs. 200/-

Cyberwit.net
HIG 45 Kaushambi Kunj, Kalindipuram
Allahabad - 211011 (U.P.) India
http://www.cyberwit.net
Tel: +(91) 9415091004
E-mail: info@cyberwit.net

www.ingramcontent.com/pod-product-compliance
Lightning Source LLC
Chambersburg PA
CBHW050026170726
48282CB00025B/560

* 9 7 8 9 3 9 5 2 2 4 7 1 0 *